BEADING

on Fabric

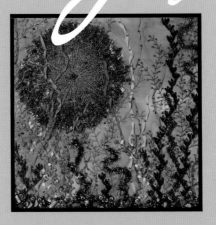

Encyclopedia of Bead Stitch Techniques

LARKIN JEAN VAN HORN

INTERWEAVE.
interweavestore.com

Over the years, my students have asked me to write this book. And so, with great affection and gratitude, I dedicate it to them. They have been good company!
—Larkin Jean Van Horn

Photography: Joe Coca
Photo styling: Ann Swanson
Cover and interior design: Paulette Livers
Illustrations: G. Armour Van Horn

Interweave Press LLC
201 East Fourth Street
Loveland, CO 80537-5655 USA
interweavestore.com

Printed in China through Asia Pacific Offset

Library of Congress Cataloging-in-Publication Data

Van Horn, Larkin, 1951-
  Beading on fabric : encyclopedia of bead stitch techniques Larkin Van Horn, author.
    p. cm.
  Includes index.
  ISBN 978-1-59668-004-3
  1. Beadwork. I. Title.
  TT860.V36 2006
  746.5—dc22
                                    2006000746

10 9 8 7 6 5 4 3

acknowledgments

At the very top of this list has to be my husband, Van. Not only does he support all of my harebrained ideas, he lends his incredible wealth of knowledge to help me get my ideas off the ground. All of the graphics you see in this book were done by him, after I had scribbled what I wanted on a napkin or scrap of paper and asked him to "make it look good!" He surely did, and I am immensely grateful.

Anne and Debra, the other two-thirds of the Three Uppity Women, have been my sounding boards, proofreaders, and cheer squad on this and other projects. Without their willing and astute assistance, I'd still be back at square one. Thanks. I needed that!

In addition to the folks at the local fabric and bead shops, who offer support and shopping assistance, the gals at the hardware store are also gracious about letting me ransack their paint chips for planning purposes. These are the kind of friends we need!

Special thanks goes to my friend Sherrill Kahn, for letting me use her gorgeous fabric to illustrate choosing a color palette. Hers is the kind of fabric that jumps off the rack and into my arms and begs me to take it home.

I did my first little bit of beading in 1972—my wedding dress. Since then, I have been privileged to view the work of many talented people, not only in the beading world, but also in the quilting, embroidery, and wearable-art worlds. Phenomenal beadwork can be found on garments for the stage, screen, and Mardi Gras, as well as the Bernina Fashion Show and the couture runways around the world. The art-quilting community is bubbling over with artists using beads on their quilts, which are exhibited in galleries, museums, and quilt shows. Everywhere I go, I find inspiration. Some of the folks whose beadwork I have admired over the years are (in no particular order): Valerie Campbell-Harding, Pamela Watts, Mimi Holmes, Mary Ann Hickey, NanC Meinhardt, David Chatt, Connie Lehman, Megan Noelle, Margaret Ball, Nancy Eha, Andrea Stern, Robin Atkins, Rebekah Hodous, Barbara McLean, Virginia Blakelock, Carol Perrenoud, and the list could go on and on. I am indebted to them for sharing their work with the rest of us.

And of course, all the good folks at Interweave Press, who took my little booklet and encouraged me to expand it into what it is today.

contents

introduction

Way back in the dawn of time, when dirt was new and dinosaurs roamed the earth, I got interested in beads. Like a lot of kids, I had a brief flirtation with archeology and wondered where they came from and who thought them up in the first place. Really, though, my main interest was that they sparkled. They were pretty. They were fun to run your fingers through. My husband, who puts up with my serious bead addiction with wry humor, likes to say that I am part raven, since I am attracted to bright, shiny objects. Okay. I can live with that. Most of my youthful experience with beads was in the jewelry boxes of my mother and grandmothers, where I also found those little bits of heaven—rhinestones! But that's another story.

Over the years, I've done a lot of embroidery and needlework of one type or another. Adding beads to the mix seemed to be a natural progression. Later, when I got interested in quilting and wearable art, beads were absolutely a requirement! And if I'm going to make a wonderful garment, well, it simply has to have wonderful jewelry to go with it!

I was basically self-taught when it came to beading and, in fact, didn't really know much about what I was doing. I only knew that I was having a good time, and folks seemed to like it. Then I got talked into sending a garment off to a traveling exhibition. I sewed and beaded like mad, and off it went. A year and a half later the garment came home to me, and half the beads were missing. I was heartbroken. I still haven't gone back to fix it. But it convinced me that I needed to figure out a better way to do things. I read, studied, talked to folks, took a couple of classes to clean up my technique, and now when I send a garment off for a fashion show or exhibit, I'm confident the beads will stay where I put them.

And that's what this book is all about. You'll find information about materials, techniques and stitches, the types of beads you will find available to you and suggestions for where to look, a few suggestions to make your work easier, and a finishing technique or two. Mostly you will find directions for doing the stitches in the most secure way possible, so that your beads will stay where you put them.

Also spread liberally throughout the book you will find photographs of some of my work that I hope will prove inspirational to you as you start working with the various stitches that will soon be part of your toolbox. Some of these pieces were made for exhibitions and some were made just for fun. And that's what I hope for you—that you will have fun with your newfound skills and have many happy hours of beading.

And though there isn't a chapter about ergonomics included, I can give you these few suggestions that have served me well:

- Work at a table, rather than sprawled on the sofa. Your back will thank you.
- Sit in a comfortable, adjustable chair, at the right height for your table and with sufficient support.
- Set the kitchen timer for 30 minutes, and leave the timer in the kitchen so that you have to get up to go turn it off. Your hands and eyes need the break.
- Make your breaks at least 10 minutes long. Do some basic stretches during your break, and take your eyes off those little tiny beads. They need to readjust, too.

And one final suggestion before we jump right into the good stuff: carry a sketchbook with you wherever you go. Inspiration is all around us, but life moves at a frenetic pace. Capture those good ideas before they disappear. Even if all you do is write down a potential color scheme, that can be enough to jump start a project at some later date. Digital cameras are getting smaller and easier to carry around with you. And in a pinch, most convenience stores sell those throw-away cameras, if you find yourself in need of a way to capture a moment. Don't hesitate to stop and shoot the roses! After you smell them, of course!

I wish you well on your journey and many happy hours of beading!

CHAPTER 1
Tools and Materials

Those of us who like to sew beads onto fabric have a number of things to consider before we start: what we will stitch on, what thread to use, what needle to use, and whether the fabric needs to be stabilized and with what. Basically, if you can get a needle through it, you can sew beads onto any fabric you like, but you will find some are easier to work with than others.

Figure 1. Heavyweight fabrics.

Fabric

Heavyweight fabrics have the advantage of being incredibly stable and not prone to stretching and sagging (Figure 1). Leather and Ultrasuede fall into this category. Though I choose not to work with these fabrics myself, I know a number of extremely talented bead artists who love working with them. (For my somewhat older hands, it's more work to get the needle through the fabric.) If you want to work with leather or suede, you might find a thimble helpful for pushing the needle through. If you have trouble getting a metal thimble to stay on your finger, check with your local quilting or needlework shop for a leather thimble. They seem to stay on better.

A couple of other fabrics that I put into the heavyweight category are not really "heavy" at all. But they don't stretch or sag, so this is where I put them (Figure 2). Lacy's Stiff Stuff is a polyester stabilizer designed especially for beaders. Timtex is an ultra heavyweight interfacing, originally designed for stiffening baseball cap brims, but it is enjoying great popularity among quilters for fabric bowls and boxes. Timtex is about double the thickness of Lacy's Stiff Stuff. Both of these materials can be easily cut to any shape, can be colored with paint or permanent markers, and are very easy to stitch through. They can also be covered with any lightweight fabric and be used as a backing fabric for your beading project.

Figure 2. Not really "heavy" weight.

Figure 3. Medium-weight fabrics.

Medium-weight fabrics would include things like wool, velvet, velveteen, polar fleece, drapery fabric, and upholstery fabrics (Figure 3). All fabrics in this category would have to be examined for any specific challenges, like stretch, pile, rubberized back finishes, etc. Anything with a pile will have a tendency to swallow up small beads. Testing the fabric would be a good idea. If the small beads disappear into the pile, you might want to consider adding a small sequin under each bead to control the pile and allow the bead to show. Some upholstery fabrics have been given a very tough back finish that would make stitching through it much more labor intensive. Depending on the project, it may or may not be worth the effort.

Most of the medium-weight fabrics are fairly stable, but velvet will have a tendency to stretch or sag. A stabilizer of some type would be appropriate (see following comments on stabilizers).

Lightweight fabrics come in huge varieties of style and fiber content: cottons, silks, linens, rayons, and myriad synthetics. Because they are easiest on my hands these are the fabrics most often used in my work (Figure 4). For a heavily beaded piece, I will choose my fabric to coordinate with the beads used, so that, if the fabric should show through the beading, it will not distract the eye from the bead-work.

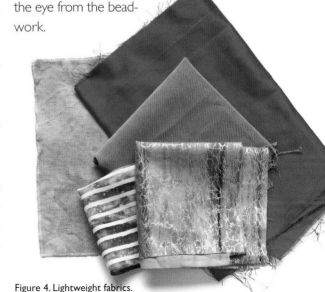

Figure 4. Lightweight fabrics.

While easy to use and wonderful to stitch on, lightweight fabrics have one problem to be overcome. Though a few beads in your hand don't feel like they weigh much, it doesn't take many before the weight of the glass on the fabric can cause sagging and stretching problems. Some sort of stabilizer will help.

Figure 5. Stabilizers.

For quilters, the logical stabilizer will be batting. My preference is a cotton or cotton-blend batting, but polyester battings will also work. There are also some lovely wool and silk battings now available.

For wearable-art artists, a light flannel or sew-in interfacing might make the most sense. My personal preference is to not use a fusible interfacing, as the "glue" adds so much additional drag on the needle and can cause the thread to fray more easily. But if the rest of your project requires the stability of a fusible interfacing, then by all means, use it. Just cut your threads a little shorter to cut down on the fraying.

For projects where added depth is not really an option, such as doll making, some types of jewelry, or beaded buttons, a layer of muslin may be all that is required.

If you are making a purse or a hat that has to hold its shape, you might consider buckram or Timtex as your stabilizer of choice (Figure 5).

Beading Thread

Everyone who works with beads will have a preference for a particular thread. Ask any room full of beaders what thread they like, and you'll get all kinds of answers. My best advice is to try everything and decide what you like to work with. That said, here's some basic information about the threads currently available to us (Figure 6).

Nymo, Nylux, C-Lon

These are all flat nylon threads, made especially for the beading world. They are sold primarily on small bobbins that are easy to carry around with you. Many colors and weights are available on the bobbins, and black and white are available on larger spools and cones. I prefer to work with "D" weight for sewing beads onto fabric and work with a doubled thread for extra stability.

Venus On The Half Shell: Day Two

Techniques: Hand-dyed fabrics, fabric collage, ribbon weaving, free machine lace, machine and hand embroidery, embellishments, beading.

Statement: Made for the Bernina Fashion Show 2002 and inspired by the Sandro Botticelli painting *The Birth of Venus*, which depicts a lovely young woman rising out of the sea on a clam shell, but eventually a girl's got to get dressed!

Figure 6. Beading threads.

"D" is a somewhat heavyweight thread, which can be a bit of a challenge to thread through the needle, but if you cut the thread at an angle using very sharp scissors, you should have an easier time of it. The ends can fray a bit, but running the thread end through beeswax helps. If no beeswax is handy, apply a little lip balm (Chap Stick, Blistex, etc.) and draw the thread end through your lips. That also keeps your lips moist! But avoid lipstick due to color transfer problems.

Since the thread is wound onto a small bobbin, it will come off with a bit of a twist, which gets worse as you get closer to the core. Just cut the thread off the bobbin, grab both ends, and give it a hard tug, which should take care of most of the problem.

Silamide

This is a round nylon thread, also made especially for beading. It is sold in short lengths on cards or on large spools. It is available in a number of colors, though fewer than the flat nylons above. I have only seen it in one weight, "A," which is about the same weight and strength as "D" weight Nymo. It is prewaxed, which makes it very easy to thread through the needle. I have had only one problem using Silamide when stitching through a very loosely bonded cotton batting. The wax on the thread caused some bearding (small tufts of batting were pulled through the top fabric to the surface). Test the batting you are using by taking a few stitches through both the batting and the top fabric. If bearding occurs, add a layer of muslin between the top and the batting.

Kevlar

A stiffer thread than either of the nylon threads, Kevlar is the stuff they make bulletproof vests from. If whatever you are making is going to get extremely heavy wear (like putting beads on your granddaughter's socks), it might be worth it to invest in Kevlar. It is available in a limited

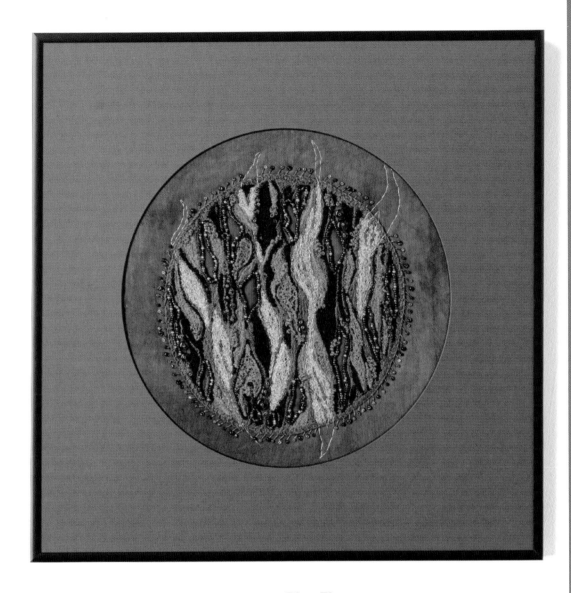

Blue Flame

(unfinished)

About 12 × 10"

Techniques: Free machine lace, hand embroidery, beading.

Statement: Lines and clusters of beading bring light to the surface of this heavily stitched piece, adding definition to the flame shapes.

variety of colors. I recommend that you not cut this with your expensive embroidery scissors. It will dull the scissors very quickly and can permanently damage them. There are some embroidery scissors on the market with serrated edges that were designed for cutting the more troublesome metallic embroidery threads, which would be useful for this.

Fire Line, Power Pro

These threads come from fishing suppliers and are now being marketed to beaders. They are very strong and extremely popular with beaders doing weaving and stringing. I use them for fringe on projects that will be out in public and vulnerable to lots of handling and wear. For beading on garments, I find they are too stiff to allow for the drape and movement I want but work well for jewelry or something that will hang on the wall. Again, don't cut this with your good scissors. Fishing supply companies sell scissors made especially for cutting Fireline, Power Pro, and Kevlar thread.

Sewing Threads

Silk is a good choice for stringing and knotting pearls. Cotton and polyester threads will shred and break more easily than the nylon beading threads, especially if they encounter beads with any rough edges. The cotton threads are also vulnerable to rotting when used with silver-lined beads.

Invisible threads can get brittle when exposed to heat. Personally, I'd rather not take any chances with all my hard work. I stick with the threads made especially for beading.

If, however, you are making a crazy quilt, and are doing lots of hand embroidery with threads like floss and pearl cotton and want to incorporate beads in with the stitching, by all means do so. Just check your beads carefully for rough edges and discard any that are of lower quality. Or consider blending in a lightweight (A or B) beading thread with the floss for strength.

Needles

There are two types of needles made specifically for beadwork: long and short (Figure 7). The long ones are great for loomwork and long fringe, but for sewing beads onto fabric I prefer the short ones. Having said that, I have had a number of students who preferred to stitch with the

Figure 7. Needles.

Pathway Through The Marsh

8.25 × 10.25"

Techniques: Hand-dyed and textured silk, machine quilting, beading, fused-glass cabochon.

Statement: Inspired by a wooden bridge through some marshland, which always seems to have something growing up between the boards.

long ones, so try both and decide which is right for you.

Beading needles are sized just like all other needles: the higher the number, the smaller the needle. Size 10 is commonly available, but sometimes the eye is too large for the bead holes. Size 12 will go through almost anything but can be a real bear to thread. I find the Size 11 suits most of the work I do.

Glue

I use a dab of glue to tack down a cabochon so it stays put while I'm beading around it. There are a number of glues available that will work just fine (Figure 8).

For smaller, lighter-weight cabochons, try Beacon's GemTac or Aileene's Jewel-It. These both dry relatively quickly, and you

Figure 8. Glues.

can be ready to bead in just a few hours.

For larger, heavier cabochons, you want something a little stronger like E-6000 or Barge Cement. These are both industrial glues, and the Barge product was originally designed for shoe repair, so it is especially good for leather work. Both of these stink to high heaven, so do the gluing outdoors or in the garage. They also should sit for 24 hours before you start beading.

It's very tempting to consider a hot glue gun for this since you could start beading almost immediately. But the hot-melt glue will be more likely to pull away from the fabric before you get the cabochon caged. So have a little patience and use something else.

If you should need to secure any knots on the surface of your work, try a tiny drop of G-S Hypo Cement to keep the knot from coming loose.

When using a loosely woven fabric, you might want to secure the edge by stitching or serging. If that's not available to you, try Fray Check or Fray Stop to control the edges.

Scissors

I am a big proponent of the idea that you should work with the best tools you can afford. This holds true especially with scis-

Journal Quilt: February 2003

11 × 8.5"

Techniques: Collage of African fabrics, machine quilting, encrusted beading.

Statement: The spirit figure was designed to complement the fabrics used in the collage.

Journal Quilt: May 2003

11 × 8.5"

Techniques: Hand-dyed and textured silk, machine quilting, encrusted beading.

Statement: The combination of textured silk and encrusted beading is an amazing tactile experience—a delight to the fingers!

Figure 9. Scissors.

sors (Figure 9). There are plenty of inexpensive scissors out there that will cut thread. I prefer to work with a pair of good quality, very sharp, very fine-pointed embroidery scissors. Mine happen to be Ginghers, but there are a number of good brands out there. Sharpness is important so that you leave a good clean end when cutting the thread off the spool. That makes it much easier to thread the needle. Fine points will allow you to get the scissors into close quarters, if needed. I find large sewing shears too big and clumsy for small, fine work.

Hoops and Frames

If what you are making is small enough to fit into a hoop or the area to be beaded can be contained in a hoop, and you are comfortable using one, do so. If you are working on a larger piece, be sure to remove the hoop whenever you stop stitching so as not to leave any permanent hoop marks. The only real problem with using a hoop is that trying to clamp a hoop over a place that has already been beaded can be problematic. Glass beads just don't "squish" between the rings like fabric does.

If what you are making absolutely must lie flat when you are finished beading, and your beading stitches tend to be a bit on the tight side (like mine), you should consider working on a frame (Figure 10).

Figure 10. Hoops and frames.

Atlantis Landscape

2.5 × 8" (3.75 × 9.5" framed)

Techniques: Encrusted beading, polymer cabochon, mounted in oak box lid.

Statement: I am fascinated by the idea of a lost continent and what that might look like.

Needleworkers use frames all the time, and the components are available at most needlework and craft shops, so making up a frame in the size you need is quite simple. Use flat needlepoint or quilter's tacks to secure the fabric and stabilizer to the frame and start beading.

Working with a frame can get a bit awkward, especially in the larger sizes, so get some help. I like the quick release clamps available at the hardware store. The newer ones have rubberized jaws so the clamp won't hurt your tabletop, though you should still protect your table from any rubbing by the frame. Simply clamp the frame to the table, and you will have both hands free to work. You will have to

unclamp to tie off a thread, but this is still a far kinder-to-your-hands approach than trying to grip a larger frame with one hand and stitch with the other. I've worked with a 24"-square frame in this manner, and it worked just fine.

Storage

I can't begin to tell you how many different ways I've seen people store their beads. Everyone has a favorite, and eventually you will figure out what works for you (Figure 11). The larger your collection of beads becomes, the more important compact storage becomes.

Beads are sold in hanks, bags, tubes of various sizes, boxes, and on strings. Tubes and

Figure 11. Types of storage.

boxes are fun to look at, easy to use, and easy to see into. The problem is that when you get down to $\frac{1}{2}$" of beads in a 6" tube, you have a lot of wasted space. Hanks and strings are vulnerable to breakage and beads spilling all over the place. And some of the bags that beads come in are glassine, brittle, and stapled at the top so they can't be resealed.

My solution to the storage problem is to buy resealable bags in three sizes: 2 × 2", 2 × 3", and 3 × 3". That seems to take care of all my needs. The beads are then sorted by color and placed in divided plastic boxes from a storage-supply shop, and the boxes are labeled and stored on bookshelves within easy reach of my beading table.

Work Space

I have a 6' table dedicated to my beading projects that sits right behind the sofa in the living room. That way I can listen to movies while I bead. (Hey, I know when to look up for the good parts, and then I can go back to beading!) The table is big enough that I can leave several projects out at all times and work on whichever takes my fancy. The table top is completely covered with Velux, an inexpensive blanket material, to keep the beads from rolling all over the place or onto the floor. I bought a twin-sized blanket and cut it to size for the table. The leftovers were cut up into mats to take with me to classes or bead society meetings. I like to work with the beads right on the table, but

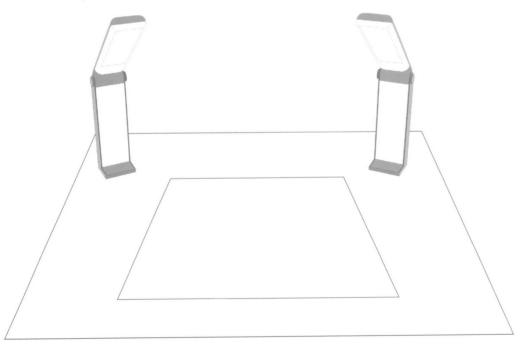

Figure 12. Table with lamp placement.

many beaders like to use a variety of bowls, dishes, or trays.

Light is essential for anyone doing small, detailed work, and beaders are no exception. I have two flip-up lights on my table, angled so they direct light at my work area from two different directions (Figure 12). This effectively eliminates most shadows on the work surface and makes it much easier on my eyes than working in the shadows.

I have a pincushion on the table for beading needles only. I found I was losing a lot of needles on the floor until I had a place to stick them for color changes. If that seems just too old fashioned for you, you could try a magnetic needle case or some other fun thing.

Figure 13. Traveling bead case.

Traveling With Beadwork

There is no way in the world that I would want to travel with my entire beading collection. I'd need two sherpas and a pack mule! But when I am on the road, I like to have a project or two with me for evenings in the hotel or breaks in the conference. Packing up a project to take with you should be fairly simple, but some thought needs to go into your packing (Figure 13).

Since 9/11, the items you can take on an airplane are more restricted. You might decide that beading on the plane is not for you and pack everything in your checked luggage. But if you want to try beading on the plane or in the waiting area before boarding your flight, you might want to buy some blunt-tipped scissors like the ones we all used in kindergarten. Even though the regulations have changed to allow sharp scissors on board, you may still want to pack your good embroidery scissors in your checked bags. Put the blunt-tipped scissors right on top, so the screeners can easily see that they are not dangerous. That can save you having your bags rummaged through. I've never had a problem with my beading needles being questioned in the United States.

You'll also need a portable work surface. The little Velux mats are fine for a table in the hotel but something more stable is

Morning Meditations With Mickey

17 × 20"

Techniques: Fused appliqué, machine quilting, beading.

Statement: This piece is the result of guided imagery exercises, and the beads lend focus and light to the overall work.

needed for the airport or train station. My travel case is made out of a zippered book cover, sold at book and discount stores. You can go with an inexpensive cloth cover or spring for a good leather cover. Mine is cheap and not particularly attractive, but it does the job. I glued two little Velux mats to the insides so I have two surfaces for pouring out beads to work with. On the outside of the cover is a zippered pocket where I keep my tools, and the fabric and beads can stay inside the book cover when not being used. When open, the book cover is just the right size for the tray table on the plane. And if you should run into turbulence on the flight, you can just slap the two sides together and zipper everything up so you don't lose anything. You may have a mess to clean up later, but you won't lose anything. Also,

think about requesting a window seat so you don't have people jostling your elbow while you try to stitch.

Handy But Not Essential

Let's face it—getting all those little beads back into the baggies or tubes can be a real pain. A tool would be nice, and, fortunately, there are several styles available (Figure 14). Check your local bead shop or online source. On the other hand, in a pinch, go to the kitchen and see if you have something languishing in the bottom of a drawer that might do the job until the right tool comes along.

From time to time, you'll come across a bead that has a less than generous hole size. Your needle went through just fine the first time but on the second pass, it has become stuck. If backing out and removing the offending bead is going to cause you a lot of stress, perhaps breaking the bead is the answer. This can be accomplished with a pair of needle-nose pliers, but you run the risk that crushing the broken glass into the thread will cut the thread. A better option is a crimping tool used by folks making jewelry (Figure 15). It has a specially designed jaw that will crush the bead but not to the point of cutting the thread. And remember, these are glass shards, and you should protect your eyes when breaking a bead.

Figure 14. Scoops.

Figure 15. Crimp tool and needle-nose pliers.

Transitions

6 × 2.5" + strap

Techniques: Encrusted beading, fused-glass cabochon.

Statement: From my talisman collection, this piece was made at a time when life seemed to be in flux, in need of resolution.

CHAPTER 2
Beads

When it comes to beading on fabric, we have an unbelievably huge selection available to us. Colors, sizes, shapes, and finishes abound out there in bead world! All we have to do is decide. And that can be a problem. I tend to want at least a dozen of everything I see, but the landlord would probably object if I spent the rent money on beads every month. So here's some information on the basics that might be helpful to you as you make your decisions.

Seed and bugle beads come to us from India, China, the Czech Republic, and Japan, and each country has its own standards for uniformity of size, shape, and hole size. The beads from India and China can be quite irregular, and this will lead to some very organic texture in your work. That can be good or bad, depending on the look you are after. The Czech beads are more uniform but can still vary significantly from bead to bead. The most uniform in size and shape come from Japan and, as a result of their higher standards, are more expensive.

Seed Beads

These are the basic backbone of beading on fabric. They are the simple, round bits of glass with holes in them that will be a major component of your work. Seed beads are manufactured by blowing out a long cane of glass, then chopping them to size. They are then heated to make them round and smooth.

Seed beads come in a number of sizes from 0° to 24°. (The higher the number, the smaller the bead.) The largest seed

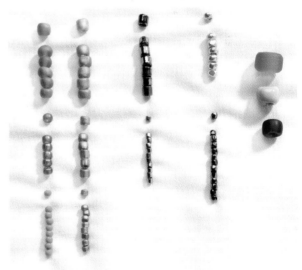

Figure 1. Seed beads.

beads are sometimes called "Crow" beads, and the size 5°, 6°, and 8° are sometimes called "Pony" beads. Sizes 10°, 11°, and 12° are what most people are referring to when they say "seed beads." Sizes 14° and 15° are pretty small but are really useful for holding individual sequins onto the surface of the fabric. I've seen the really tiny beads, sizes 20°–24°, but my eyes aren't good enough to use them.

Charlottes (also called "true cuts" or "one cuts") are seed beads with one or more flat sides, which gives them extra sparkle. Though these terms are often used interchangeably, technically, size 13° one cuts are charlottes, and size 11° one cuts are called true cuts.

Figure 2. Bugle beads.

Delicas (also called "Antique" or "Delicious") are incredibly uniform, cylindrical beads from Japan, with very thin walls and large holes. They look pretty small, but because of the large holes they are easy to work with. They are available in size 8° and size 11° (Figure 1).

Bugle Beads

These are the long tubular beads sized to coordinate with the seed beads. They are manufactured the same way as seed beads but are not fired to round them out. That means that the edges are sharp and will easily cut through your beading thread. (Don't ask me how I know!) I have heard a number of suggestions for ways to eliminate the problem of sharp edges, including someone who suggested that the ends of each bugle bead be painted with clear fingernail polish. The best solution I can think of is to always use a seed bead on both ends of the bugle bead. That way, when your thread goes back into the fabric, it rests on a smooth edge rather than a sharp one.

Bugle beads are sized in millimeters and come as short as 2mm (Figure 2). The very long ones can be vulnerable to breakage on a garment and once broken can cut the thread. But they look great in fringe! Remember to use a needle long enough to go all the way through the bead.

I Went To The Woods

6 × 3.5" + strap

Techniques: Encrusted beading, polymer cabochon,
fused-glass drop.

Statement: From my talisman collection, inspired by
the writings of Henry David Thoreau.

Triangles, Cubes, and Hexes

Like the names suggest, these are glass beads cut from three-, four- or six-sided canes.

There are two different styles of triangles available (Figure 3). One has very sharp angles and one very soft angles. Both styles are available in two different sizes. Watch the ones with sharp angles for equally sharp edges and take appropriate precautions.

Cubes are sold in 2mm, 3mm, and 4mm sizes, and the hexes in 8°, 11°, and 14° sizes. With the exception of the 2mm cubes, they have nice big holes and are easy to work with. They also create wonderful texture amidst the round seeds and bugles.

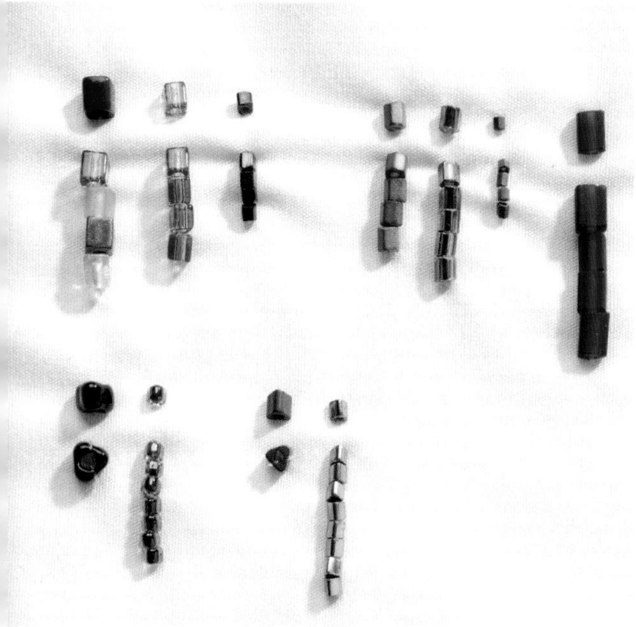

Pressed Glass

The variety of shapes available in this category is somewhat mindboggling—teardrops, rondelles, pyramids, stars, hearts, even tennis shoes (Figures 4a and 4b)! You name it, you can probably find it somewhere. Some shapes will work better on the surface of fabric than others, and those others can be used in fringe. I learned a lot about what various shapes are called by hanging out on eBay and reading the descriptions and looking at the pictures. (I also spent a fair amount of money that way, but we won't go into that!) Anyway, that's where I learned that a round, flat, saucer-like bead with a hole in the center is called a "rondelle" and that a bead that looks about the same with a hole near the edge is called a "lentil." Who knew?

Faceted and Fire Polished

These are glass beads that have been cut by hand or machine or fired to create multiple flat surfaces, which reflect light wonderfully (Figure 5)! The sparkle factor of your work goes way up when using faceted beads. There are quite a number

Figure 3. Cubes, hexes, and triangles.

Figure 4a. Rondelles and lentils.

Figure 4b. Pressed glass.

Figure 5. Faceted and fire-polished beads.

Figure 6. Lampworked beads.

of shapes available as faceted beads and lots of colors. For maximum sparkle, take a look at Swarovski crystals. You pay more for all that glitz, but nothing shines like Swarovski!

Lampworked

Lampworked beads are made one at a time by a bead artist working with rods of glass and a torch (Figure 6). They can be simple or extremely complex; small and of limited color range or very large using every color imaginable. You can buy inexpensive lampworked beads from India at bead and craft shops, and you can also spend hundreds of dollars for one bead from the artist who made it. Though usually used in jewelry, you might find some special lampworked glass to include in your next project.

Gemstone and Gemstone Chips

This is an area where a little caution is called for. First, they look great, and you can be tempted to put off paying the phone bill in order to acquire a bunch! But also, not everything that looks like a real gemstone is a real gemstone. Any reputable bead shop will tell you if the material is enhanced, man-made, or reconstructed in any way. But what if you are shopping at a street market and dealing with strangers? Let the price be your guide. If it looks like turquoise, but is

Raven's Treasure

18 × 24"

Techniques: Fabric collage, machine and hand embroidery, embellishments, beading.

Statement: My husband likes to say that I must be part raven, because I am attracted to bright shiny things! That must be why I'm a beader!

Figure 7. Gemstone and gemstone chips.

Figure 8. Shells.

priced like plastic, leave it on the table. On the other hand, there's no reason not to use an enhanced or man-made stone or stone chip if you like the look, and it's what you need for the project you have in mind. Just be aware of what you are getting (Figure 7).

One other caution: quite a few man-made or enhanced stones have been dyed. Testing for colorfastness may be in order, especially if the item will get any significant amount of wear or exposure to direct sunlight. See notes on colorfastness, page 38.

Shells

Many bead shops have shells and shell pieces that have been drilled for use in beading (Figure 8). Just be careful of sharp edges that might cut your thread. Another source of shells for beading would be your local thrift shop. They frequently have necklaces made of shells that can be taken apart and the shells used in your projects.

If you want to drill holes in shells you might pick up at the beach, a Dremel tool will come in handy. You'll want to work wet to keep the dust level down, and wear a dust mask to keep from inhaling any errant shell dust. Also, you'll need to stabilize the shell in some way so it doesn't move around while you are drilling. Try pushing the shell into a lump of polymer or modeling clay.

Get Me To The Train On Time

Techniques: Fabric collage and weaving, machine and hand embroidery, embellishments, beading.

Statement: Made for the Bernina Fashion Show 2004 and inspired by the film Hello, Dolly!, this ensemble combines nineteenth-century styling and twenty-first-century techniques, with plenty of beads sprinkled into the mix.

Figure 9. Pearls.

Pearls

Some of my favorite things, and currently a major drain on my pocketbook, are pearls. And with the wide variety of sizes, shapes, and colors on the market, it's no wonder (Figure 9)! Treat them like any other beads when sewing them onto fabric. Pay attention to the colorfastness of those remarkable colors and enjoy! You may run into a string of pearls that have been drilled with very tiny holes, which may make it difficult to get the needle through twice. There is a tool called a bead reamer that will come in handy for making the holes a little larger.

Cabochons

Cabochon is a French jeweler's term, usually referring to a gemstone with a flat back for putting into a jewelry setting of some kind. For our purposes, we will say that a cabochon (or cab) is anything with a flat side that can be placed on the surface of the fabric. And I do mean anything (Figure 10). Fused glass, beach glass, stone slices, driftwood, bottle caps, polymer, pottery, buttons, coins, mirror, shell, fossils, you name it, cabochons provide a focal point for the beadwork around it and can be the inspiration for color scheme or style of beading.

There are so many wonderful buttons available, both new and antique, that it seems a shame that so many of them are languishing in jars and boxes. Why not

A bead reamer.

Figure 10. Cabochons.

design a project around one smashing button? If the button has holes through it, attaching it to the fabric is easily accomplished. If, however, the button has a shank, it can be a problem to get it to lie down flat on the surface. Sometimes the shank can be removed, which takes care of the problem. But many antique buttons, and even some modern buttons, have shanks that cannot be removed without destroying them. The solution is simple but a little scary. (Sit down. Take a deep breath.) Take an awl or ice pick and poke a hole in the fabric and stabilizer where the button/cabochon will be placed. Apply a little glue to the back of the button and push the shank through the hole. Roll up a small piece of muslin and push it through the shank. Then stitch the muslin to the stabilizer and allow the glue to dry before you start stitching (Figure 11). Note to quilters: You can do this before you put the back on the quilt so the shank doesn't show out the back. The glue will keep the fabric from fraying.

Figure 11. Button shank through fabric.

Finishes and Colorfastness

Beads come with many surface finishes, and some finishes have many different names. I don't honestly care what it's called. I buy what I like, according to what I need for the project at hand. But there are a few finishes that you need to pay attention to.

Dyed or Color-Lined: These transparent glass beads have had a color added after the bead was finished. The color is either applied to the outside of the bead or through the hole. Either way, these beads are vulnerable to color fading, rubbing off, or bleeding onto the cloth if they get wet. Most reputable bead shops will tell you if a bead is dyed (if they know). They should also let you take a bead or two out to the parking lot where you can test them with a little nail polish remover on a paper towel. If they are going to bleed, you can still use them but not on anything that will be washed, dry cleaned, or be handled a lot. If the project will go into a frame or hang on the wall, just keep it out of direct sun to minimize fading.

Metallic or Galvanized: These opaque glass beads have been coated with a metallic paint that has been baked on (Figure 12). You can depend on the finish flaking off if the beads get any wear at all. So

Fertile Fields

5.5 × 5.5" (8 × 8" framed)

Techniques: Encrusted beading, fused-glass cabochon.

Statement: Inspired by the land forms and patterns

seen from the window of an airplane.

Bracelet with chipped beads.

what once was a beautiful metallic copper will become a truly ugly battleship gray. Don't take any chances with these. Put the work in a frame and hang it on the wall. (Don't ask me how I know!)

Silver-Lined: These beads give you all kinds of glitz and are some of my personal favorites. And with all the synthetic foils available these days, it is unlikely that you will run into very many that are truly lined with silver. However, if you are working with vintage beads or treasures from the thrift shop, you never know. The silver can tarnish and the beads can become dull and lifeless. Also, if you have sewn the beads on with cotton thread instead of nylon beading thread, the cotton can rot from the tarnishing of the silver.

Figure 12. Galvanized beads.

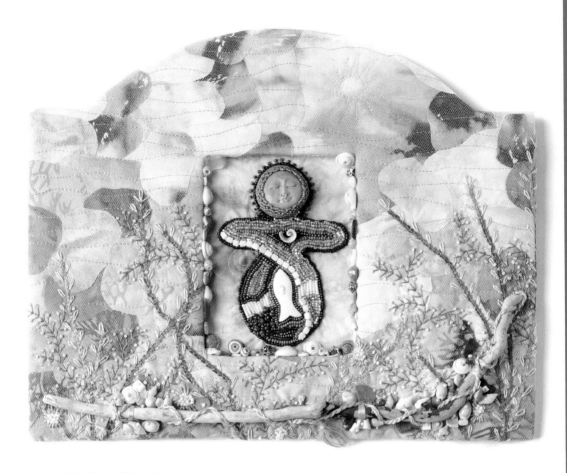

A Gift from The Sea

10.25 × 13"

Techniques: Fabric collage, machine quilting, hand embroidery, encrusted beading, mounted on foam board.

Statement: Inspired by Anne Morrow Lindbergh's book of the same name, this piece includes one of my spirit figures.

Beaded Buttons

Various 1.25" to 3"

Techniques: Encrusted beading on button forms.

Statement: I make beaded buttons in hotel rooms at
night when I'm on the road. Eventually the right
project will come along, and the button will get
added.

An Unnamed Saint

17" point to point

Techniques: Encrusted beading, porcelain face by
Diana Briegleb.

Statement: Inspired by the writings of Madeleine
L'Engle, and created during an artist residency.

Emerging II: A Pale Reflection

20 × 17.5"

Techniques: Fused appliqué, machine quilting, beading.

Statement: This abstract, organic form gains focus
with the addition of beads.

CHAPTER 3
Getting Started

When it comes to sewing beads onto fabric, there are very few rules. Since I am a fly-by-the-seat-of-my-pants gal, this is a good thing! There are, however, a few suggestions that might make your work go more smoothly.

The Rules

I always use two strands of thread when sewing beads onto fabric. From time to time, you will get a bead with a rough spot in the hole that can eventually wear the thread away. If you have two strands and one lets go, you still have one holding on until you can make a repair. This is especially important if the beads are going onto a garment that will get some wear, a quilt that will be traveling to exhibits or shows, or a decorator pillow on your sofa.

When possible, try to match the color of the thread as closely as you can to the color of the beads (Figure 1). Or, as another option, match the thread to the color of the fabric. One of the things we want is for the beads to get the attention—not the threads they were sewn on

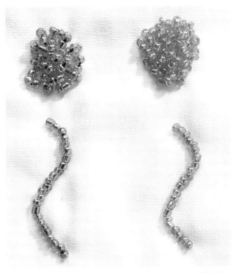

Figure 1. Stitch sample with contrasting thread (left) and matching thread (right).

Figure 2. Line drawn, partially stitched.

with. An exception to this might be on a crazy quilt where the beads are part of the stitching created by the embroidery floss or pearl cotton.

If you need the beads to follow a particular line or design, go ahead and draw the line on the fabric (Figure 2). That's not cheating—that's making the best possible use of the resources at hand and helping you avoid having to rip things out later. You will be beading right on the line, so don't worry about it showing. You can use a disappearing pen, fabric pencil, or tailor's chalk for this purpose, but my favorite is a big box of colored pencils. I can always find a color that will show up on the fabric, they are easy to keep sharpened, and are readily available.

How Many Beads To Use

Students ask me all the time how I decided how many beads to use on a particular project. There's no easy answer. Or perhaps there is. Use as many beads as are needed for the look you want—no more and no less.

I have a theory that there are three basic approaches to putting beads on fabric: the minimalist approach, all things in moderation, and encrusted.

The Minimalist Approach

This approach means just what it says. The beads are there only for a little twinkle. The only purpose of the beads is to catch the light and draw the viewer in. This would be something like a scattering of crystalline seed beads across a night sky to emphasize the stars or some opaque mustard-colored seed beads as corn kernels in a farmyard scene.

All Things in Moderation

In this approach, the beads are there for a reason—to emphasize a line, to fill space, to point to the focus of the piece. These might be lines of seed and bugle beads as rays of the sun or lines of pearl seed beads along the folds of a gown. The centers of flowers can be filled with beads for texture.

Encrusted

Ah! This is where I feel most at home. The beads are not just filling space—they are the whole reason for making the piece in the first place! The more the merrier, I say! And much of the time the fabric ends up not showing at all. The beads in this category can be larger and more tightly packed together than in the other two categories, which brings up the problem of weight. When heavily encrusting something with beads, it is very important that the right stabilizer be used and that the

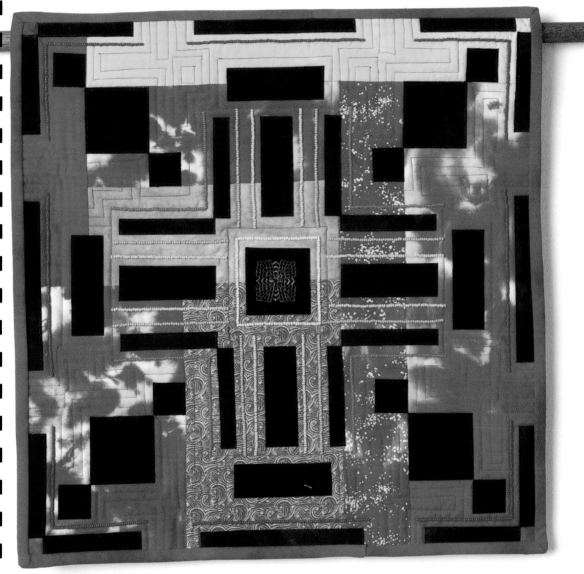

Sun Sign

16.25 × 16.25"

Techniques: Machine piecing, fused appliqué, machine quilting, beading.

Statement: A somewhat assymetrical interpretation of a Tibetan mandala, the beading helps define the lines and stabilize the structure.

finishing techniques accommodate the weight of the beads (see page 10). Some experimentation might be required.

Choosing Your Color Scheme

I only include this because I get asked a lot. There are plenty of books out there about formal color theory, if that's what you're after. And learning formal color theory can go a long way in helping you solve any problems that come up with a project. If your project lacks punch, you can figure out what color might perk it up by studying the color wheel.

But if you are the least bit timid about choosing a color scheme for your next project, take yourself on a field trip to a fabric or quilting store. Spend some time browsing through the fabrics, especially the multicolored prints, and pay attention to which ones draw your eye. Most fabric stores will sell you as little as ⅛ of a yard of fabric, which you can then take to the bead shop. Be prepared to make

Figure 3. Beads, fabric, and paint chips.

Star Gazer

16.25 × 16.25"

Techniques: Machine piecing and quilting, fused appliqué, woven silk ribbons, hand embroidery, couched threads, covered washers, beading.

Statement: One of my small spirit pieces, enhanced with embellishments and beading.

some adjustments in shade and tone. While there are literally hundreds of bead colors available, there will always be more variety possible when blending inks and paints.

Another place for a field trip would be the hardware or home decorating store. Paint chips can be very helpful when trying to put colors together (Figure 3). Especially if what you will be creating are things like throw pillows, curtain tiebacks, or lamp shades to go with your newly painted walls. Also, if you are making something for a friend, having her send you paint chips can solve all the problems of figuring out just what she means when she says something like "teal and aubergine."

Notes For Wearable-art Artists

In most cases, what you are making will be lined after the beading is completed. That's a very good thing. The last thing you want is to be catching your fingernails on the exposed beading threads and possibly causing a problem with the stitches. If you are stitching on a ready-made garment that doesn't have a lining, consider adding one for the safety of your beading. Another option would be to fuse some featherweight interfacing over the beading stitches. If the inside of the garment might show, consider fusing a decorative patch over the beading stitches.

Placement of the beads is very important. You don't want to be sitting on your beads, for obvious reasons. But another area to be aware of is your back. If you are making a jacket that you will wear to the opera or theatre, you don't want to use large beads that protrude off the surface of the jacket in an area that you will be leaning against for three hours. Move the large beads up to the shoulder area or on the front of the jacket.

Seat belts are wonderful lifesaving devices, but they can be hard on your beaded garments. If it's a jacket or vest, take it off while you travel to your destination or wrap a shawl around the affected area. If it's a dress or blouse, put on a coat or sweater to protect the beads from being rubbed by the seat belt. The same goes for beaded jewelry. Keep it out of harm's way or put it on when you get there.

Notes For Quilters

To bead or not to bead; that is the question. And the answer is: YES!

You have several choices of when to do the beading, and if you ask a roomful of quilters, you'll get as many different answers— each of them convinced of the absolute truth of their own method. I have my favorite approach, too, but will present a few for your consideration.

Don't Be Late For The Ball, Boys!

Techniques: Fabric collage, machine quilting, hand embroidery, beading.

Statement: Created for the Fairfield Fashion Show 2000 and inspired by tales of the Three Musketeers.

1. Sew the beads on through the top and batting, before you do the quilting. Then add the back, proceed with the quilting, and finish as desired. This works nicely if you are hand quilting, but can be problematic for machine quilting.

2. Do all the quilting through all layers of the quilt, then add the beads. If you do not want the beading stitches to show, you will have to pay particular attention to burying the knots and hiding the connecting stitches in the layers of the quilt.

3. Use the beads as the quilting stitches, as if you were hand quilting. Bury the knots and let the stitches show, as in hand quilting.

4. And my personal favorite: layer up the quilt top with batting and a piece of muslin. Do all the quilting and then proceed to the beading. When the beading is complete, add the backing fabric, which will cover up all the beading stitches and protect them from snagging. If you have used a heavy cabochon or have densely beaded any particular area, taking a few unobtrusive hand stitches through all layers in that area will help stabilize the quilt. If the quilt is very weighty, consider fusing the back onto the quilt to give it more stability as well as to prevent sagging.

Competitions, Exhibits, and Shows

If you are making your quilt to satisfy your artistic urges or to give as a gift, you can do any old thing you want. If you are going to send it out into the world to be juried and judged, you have to play by the rules. But the rules are changing from the days of the old county-fair system, where working to the same set of rules and techniques was the order of the day. These days, beads have become acceptable, just like machine quilting. And nobody seems to mind the false backs or fused backs found on heavily embellished quilts these days. So jump right in and have a good time.

Undiscovered Universe

20.25 × 20.25"

Techniques: Machine piecing and quilting, embellished
with beaded buttons.

Statement: Beaded buttons allow the beads to make
more of a statement than small individual beads.

CHAPTER 4
The Stitches

Beads On Fabric

Before we jump into the stitches, there are a few very important issues to cover: tension and excess thread. Maintaining tension is important to most of these stitches. If your tension is too loose, the stitches will wobble all over the place and be vulnerable to catching on things. If your tension is too tight, the fabric will distort. Now, if you are after an organic, crunchy look, that's great. Otherwise, be aware of how hard you are pulling those stitches. Mine tend to be on the tight side, and it's a hard habit to break.

Excess thread is sometimes a problem. If you are laying down a line of stitches and having trouble dealing with the excess thread before going back down into the

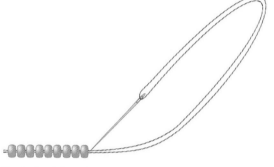

Tapping beads into place.

fabric, try this: remember that you are working with doubled thread. Hold those threads in place with one hand, then place the needle between the two threads and drag it across the fabric until it taps up against the beads. Once the beads are in place, just poke the needle through the fabric and pull it through.

Oozing Charm

16.5 × 16.5"

Techniques: Fused appliqué, machine quilting, beading.

Statement: This very 1960s-style quilt gains definition and motion with the echoing lines of bugle beads.

Seed Stitch

Similar to the embroidery stitch of the same name, a seed stitch looks just as the name suggests. Useful to represent a scattering of seeds or stars, it is also valuable as a way to fill space without obliterating the background cloth, or to add texture.

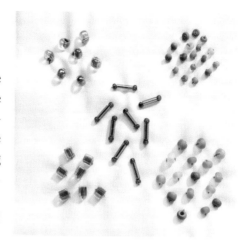

Seed stitch with various types of beads.

The key to getting the seed bead to stand up straight on the fabric is threefold:

1. Allow space for the bead between the thread entry and exit from the fabric. In other words, don't take the needle back down into the same hole it just came out of.

2. When taking the needle back down into the fabric, the needle should be perpendicular to the fabric—not at an angle.

3. Tension! With a little practice, your seed stitches will stand up just the way you want them!

Completed seed stitch.

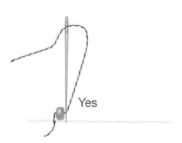

Correct needle angle.

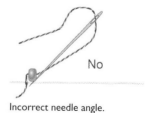

Incorrect needle angle.

Sea Dreams

10.25 × 8.25"

Techniques: Hand-dyed and textured silk, machine quilting, beading, fused-glass cabochon.

Statement: After a stay on the coast, I awoke with a vision in my head of a chambered nautilus as the moon.

Moss Stitch (Mossing)

The moss stitch is a distant cousin of the seed stitch. It is used for filling a space with lots of organic texture. Instead of a single seed bead, pick up three. Take the needle back down into the fabric about one bead width away from the entry point and pull up tight. The two outer beads should lay down hole-up on the fabric, not quite touching. The center bead should stand up, nested in the crack between the other two beads, but not touching the fabric. These stitches should be clustered close together, with the direction of the stitches changed every time for maximum impact.

For added variety and texture, try substituting a gemstone chip or tiny teardrop for the center bead. For a more sea-urchin look, substitute long dagger beads for the center.

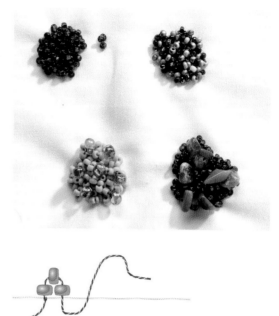

Single moss stitch.

Grouped moss stitches.

Here's My Heart

5 × 3.5" + strap

Techniques: Encrusted beading.

Statement: This little doll is beaded both sides and
assembled using the picot edge stitch to join the sides
before stuffing.

Lazy Stitch

Once called the "lazy squaw stitch," and occasionally called the "lane stitch," this stitch is used extensively in Native American bead embroidery. Short straight lines of beads are laid down on the fabric to create basket weave and other geometric patterns.

When laying down the lines of beads, do not bring the needle up right next to where you just entered the fabric with the previous stitch. You will only have a few fabric threads between stitches, which may pull out at a later time. Instead, always begin your stitches at the same end, creating long diagonal stitches on the back of the work.

Due to the varying size and shapes of seed beads, you may need to adjust the number of beads used in each line to maintain a consistent width.

Basket weave in lazy stitch.

Completed line of lazy stitch.

Diagonal thread path across back of fabric.

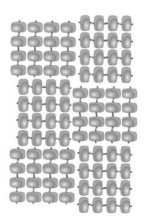

Basket weave directional diagram.

Ancient Images

12.25 × 13"

Techniques: Assemblage on foam board, beading.

Statement: This piece was inspired by the petro-glyphs. of ancient cultures, the figures gaining defini-tion from the beading.

Couching—Single Needle

Couching is used to secure a long line of beads to the fabric. The single needle method is done in two steps.

1. Bring the needle up through the fabric, string on all beads for the row, lay them in place and take the needle back into the fabric, leaving a slight amount of slack thread showing.
2. Work your way back down the row, bringing the needle up every 2 beads. Take a catch stitch over the thread and back down into the fabric just where you came up. Do not go through the beads.

The extra slack in the thread is to accommodate the catch stitches between the beads. Guessing how much slack to leave takes practice. And it can be a bit tricky spacing the beads out along the thread as you couch, but with practice, this can become a useful stitch in your repertoire.

Couching for straight or curved lines.

Single-needle couching.

Americans United

17.25 × 8.5"

Techniques: Fused collage, hand-made paper column, machine quilting, beading.

Statement: Created for the America: From The Heart touring exhibit following September 11, 2001. There is one bead set for every person on the four airplanes involved in the terrorist attacks.

Couching—Double Needle

Double-needle couching works on the same general principle as single-needle couching, however, there is no need to guess how much slack to allow. The trick here is to keep your two threads from getting tangled up!

1. Bring the first needle up from the back and string on all the beads for the row. Don't take the needle back down into the fabric. Instead, park it out of the way on another area of the fabric.
2. Bring the second needle up between the second and third beads of the line and take a catch stitch over the thread. Continue down the line, taking catch stitches every 2 beads, making sure all of the slack is taken up between the beads to eliminate gaps.
3. When the line is complete, take both needles to the back and knot them off.

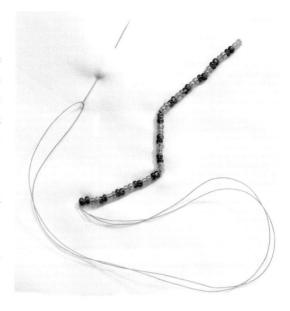

Direction changes are easy to control with double-needle couching.

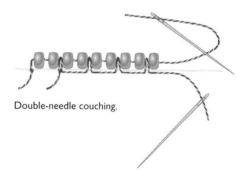

Double-needle couching.

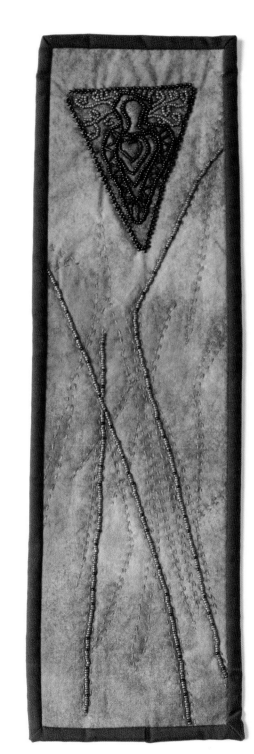

Desert Spirit

17.75 × 5.5"

Techniques: Hand-dyed and discharged cotton, hand quilting, beading.

Statement: Outline beading brings definition to the spirit figure, which was printed with a hand-carved stamp.

Backstitch

By far my most used bead embroidery stitch, backstitch is useful for both line and fill patterns.

1. Bring the needle up, string on 4 beads, lay them on the fabric and snug them up to eliminate gaps. Take the needle back down into the fabric. Like the seed stitch, try to take the needle down perpendicular to the fabric, or the end beads may bow out.
2. Bring the needle back up between the second and third beads and take the needle through the third and fourth beads again. *Do not* go back into the fabric at this point. Instead, pick up 4 more beads, go back into the fabric, and repeat the backstitching process until the line is complete.

Once you get the pattern of the stitch, a rhythm will develop and this will start to go very quickly. Also, four is not a magic number. This stitch can also be done with 3 or 5 beads, always going through the last 2 beads added. If there are more than 5 beads the line will start to get unstable.

If you need a specific line or shape, draw it on the fabric.

Backstitch.

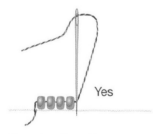

Yes

Correct needle position.

No

Incorrect needle position.

New Beginnings

6 × 3" + strap

Techniques: Encrusted beading, raku cabochon.

Statement: From my talisman collection, the cabochon is a broken pottery shard that I rescued after the pot blew up in the kiln.

Bugle Bead Pathways

Let's face it—bugle beads have bad manners! Because of the way they are made, the edges are sharp and will cut through your beading thread with little or no provocation. You can switch to Kevlar or Power Pro thread or paint the ends of each bead with nail polish. But why not just add a seed bead to either end of the bugle bead? Your mantra for working with bugle beads will be: always go into and out of a seed bead.

The Long, Skinny Line

1. Thread on a seed-bugle-seed combination, take the needle back into the fabric, and come back up at the beginning of the line again. Go back through all three beads to stabilize the line.
2. Like backstitch, now add 4 beads (bugle-seed-bugle-seed) and take the needle back into the fabric. To complete the stitch, take the needle up through the fabric and through the last 3 beads (seed-bugle-seed) and add 4 more beads. Repeat as needed to complete the line.

Bugle beads: long and skinny.

Stabilize the beginning of the line.

The long, skinny line.

The Long, Fat Line

Still working with a seed-bugle-seed combination, the beads are lined up like paving stones. Like lazy stitch, this pathway will have long diagonal stitches on the back as you lay down the rows. If you need a perfectly straight line, I suggest you draw it on the side where you will begin each stitch. Because bugle beads can vary quite a bit in length, even if they are labeled as being the same, you may have to settle for having one straight edge and one somewhat jagged edge. To camouflage this effect, try using a gently curved line, rather than a straight one.

Fat lines: fans and stars.

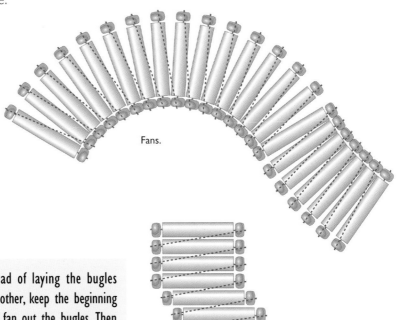

Fans.

Fat lines.

Variation: Instead of laying the bugles right next to each other, keep the beginning seeds together and fan out the bugles. Then reverse the process and fan out the beginning beads and gather the ending beads together.

Beads On Beads

Stacks

Stacks of beads will help create texture, depth, and motion in your beadwork. They are also the basis of fringe. The beads in the stacks can be all the same or can include a variety of sizes and shapes. A small seed bead at the top of the stack holds everything in place.

Bring the needle up through the fabric and string on whatever beads will comprise the stack, remembering that the top bead will need to be large enough not to slip through the hole of the bead directly under it. Take the needle back down through the stack of beads except the top bead and into the fabric. Pull it up tight, and the stack should stand right up. If you miss taking the needle through any of the beads on the way back down, the stack will kink.

This method is also useful for applying single sequins. Make sure that the size of the bead does not completely obscure the sequin. In fact, this is a good place to use smaller, size 14° or 15°, seed beads.

Stacks.

Rondelle and seed bead.

Several seed beads.

Sequin and seed bead.

Bugle and seed bead.

More Beaded Buttons

Various 1.25" to 2"

Techniques: Encrusted beading on button forms.

Basic Fringe

Though usually thought of as adorning a hem, scarf, or edge of jewelry, the possibilities of using fringe as a textural element on any beaded work are endless. Remember that you can use any variety of beads in your fringe that you wish.

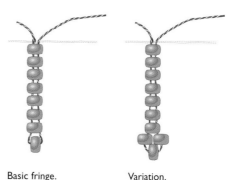

Basic fringe.   Variation.

Bring the needle out of the fabric, string beads the length of the fringe plus 1 seed bead. Ignoring the final seed bead, take the needle all the way back up through the string of fringe beads and back into the fabric. Pull up tightly, and knot after every string of fringe. This may seem like an annoying and unnecessary step, but it could save you a lot of grief if the fringe should catch on something. Better to lose one strand than several.

Variation: A fun variation of this would involve finishing the line of fringe with 3 seed beads instead of 1. When you are ready to go back up through the string, leave 3 seed beads at the bottom instead of 1. When pulled up tightly, they will look something like moss stitch at the end of the fringe and will add texture.

End Beads—Vertical Holes

There are many beads that make wonderful endings for fringe: leaves, flowers, teardrops, stone chips, etc. For those with vertical holes, the procedure is the same as above: string up your fringe beads, add the end bead and 1 seed bead. Then take the needle back up the fringe as before, leaving the seed bead to hold the whole thing together.

Basic fringe with vertical hole end bead.

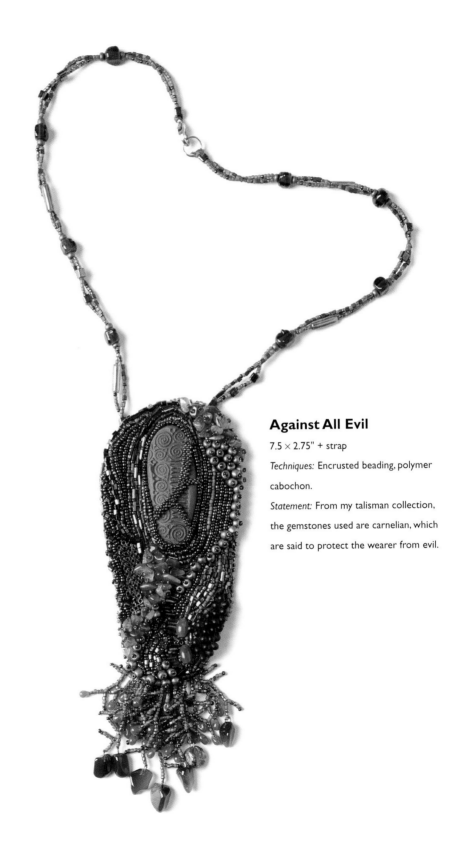

Against All Evil

7.5 × 2.75" + strap

Techniques: Encrusted beading, polymer cabochon.

Statement: From my talisman collection, the gemstones used are carnelian, which are said to protect the wearer from evil.

End Beads—Horizontal Holes

When using a teardrop, leaf, or other end bead that has a horizontal hole, a slight variation is required. In order to camouflage the thread, beads are added to both sides of the drop.

Bring the needle out of the fabric and string on beads the length of the fringe. Now add 3 seed beads, the end bead, and 3 more seed beads before returning up the core of the fringe and into the fabric. This will form a small loop at the base of the fringe. If the hole is deep into a long bead, you may need to add more than 3 seed beads to camouflage the thread. Pull up tightly and knot after each strand of fringe.

Various basic fringes.

Basic fringe with horizontal hole end bead.

Branched fringe

Branched fringe creates some of the most wonderful, lush texture around. The only tricky bit is keeping your thread from tangling up in the already finished fringe.

Bring the needle through the fabric and pick up as many beads as needed for the length of the fringe. Reverse direction, skip the end bead, and go back through 3 to 5 beads. Exit the core and * add 4 beads. Reverse direction, skip the end bead, go back through 3 beads, and into the core for 2 to 5 beads. Exit the core and repeat from * until back to the top. Take the needle into the fabric and knot after each fringe. Be sure to tighten everything up as you go along. Doing so when you get all the way to the top can be a real pain.

There are no magic numbers in branched fringe. Just as the core can be any length you wish so can the branches be any number of beads.

Branched fringe.

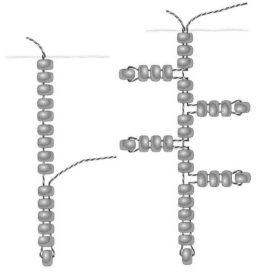

The core.   Branches added.

Variation: For added variety, try mixing up some "bead soup" of several colors or sizes of seed beads. Or, add tiny teardrops at the end of each branch. Add crystals for a touch of glitz.

Branched Fringe on the Ground

Branched fringe is great dangling off the bottom of a medallion but why stop there? It's also a fun way to add texture to the surface of your work. Bring your needle up through the fabric and create a line of branched fringe, just as previously described. When you take the needle back down into the fabric, knot it off, as usual. Now, bring the needle back up through the fabric such that you can catch the end bead of each branch and then take the needle back down through the fabric. You can have the branch lie down flat, or arch up off the surface with a little manipulation of placement. Experimentation will reveal some exciting possibilities.

Branched fringe flat on surface and arched away from surface.

Possible path for branched fringe on the ground.

Purple Is The Color Of Royalty

7.5 × 4" + strap

Techniques: Encrusted beading, raku cabochon.

Statement: From my talisman collection, this piece
was made to honor the gift of friendship.

Leaf Fringe

Like branched fringe, this adds loads of texture and movement to any piece.

Done with one or two colors—one for the branch and one for the leaf. String up as many branch beads as needed for length. * String on 7 leaf beads. Skip the end bead and go back through 1 bead only. Add 3 beads. Go through the top 2 leaf beads and 2 or 3 branch beads. Exit the branch and add 2 branch beads. Repeat from * until you reach the top.

Just like branched fringe, the leaves may be spaced as far apart as you wish along the length of the branch.

Leaf fringe using one or two colors.

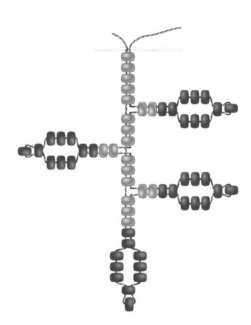

Leaf fringe thread path.

Water World

16.25 × 16.25"

Techniques: Machine piecing, raw-edge appliqué, machine quilting,
embellishment, hand embroidery, beading.

Statement: A bright, bold vision of life under the sea, with plenty
of embellishments and the twinkle of beads for light and detail.

Spiral Fringe

Another great textural fringe. Tension is very important for this one, as well as being sure you do not split the thread with the needle as you travel back up the core. Best done with the size 10°, 11°, or 12° seed beads, you might find it easier to pull up if you use a single strand of thread.

This is easier to see with two colors of beads. Bring the needle through the fabric and string on 1 bead of color A and 1 bead of color B. (Shown here as lighter and darker beads.) Repeat until you have at least eight pairs. On the reverse path, take the needle into only color A beads. When back at the top, take the needle through the fabric, pull very tightly, and knot to hold the tension. It will look like a little corkscrew.

Before and after pulling up thread.

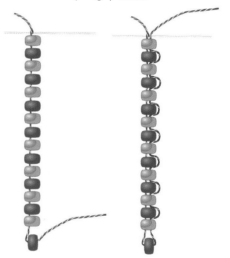

The core.   Reverse thread path.

Pulled up tight.

Kinky Fringe

Like the spiral fringe, with a slightly different formula, this is also easier to see with
two colors of beads. And again, you might
find this easier to do with size 10°, 11°, or
12° seed beads and one strand of thread.

Bring the needle through the fabric and
string on 3 beads of color A and 1 bead
of color B. (Shown here as lighter and
darker beads.) Repeat until you have four
or five sets. On the reverse path, take the
needle into only color A beads. Skip over
the color B beads. When back to the top,
take the needle through the fabric and
pull tight. Knot to hold tension.

Before and after pulling up thread.

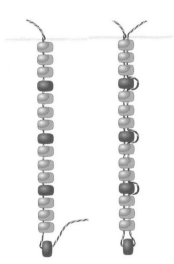

The core.   Reverse thread path.

Pulled up tight.

Netted Fringe

Imagine a fringe that looks like it came off the bottom of a Victorian lamp shade. That's netted fringe, though it can certainly be done with materials that would change the look to anything you can imagine.

This can be done with any number of colors you like but let's start with two to keep it simple. Color A will be the most prominent and color B will be shared by two sides of the fringe path. Bring the needle out of the fabric and thread on 5 beads of color A and 1 bead of color B. Repeat as many times as necessary to get the length you need.

Add 5 color A beads and the end bead (using additional beads to hide the thread if working with an end bead with a horizontal hole), take the needle back up through the 5 beads you just added, and into the first color B bead on the return path.

Add 5 color A beads, 1 color B bead, and 5 color A Beads. Now take the needle into a color B bead in the previous string, such that you create a diamond shape. Continue back up the line in this manner, creating diamonds as you go. Take the needle back into the fabric and knot it off.

Bring the needle back out through the fabric right next to the previous bead, and proceed to create diamonds connecting to the previous strings until you have made as much fringe as you need. Remember to knot off every time you go back into the fabric. This fringe is very vulnerable to catching on things. It's also tempting to little fingers!

Netted fringe.

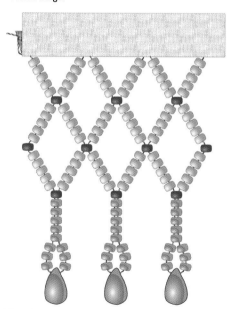

Thread path.

Twisted Fringe

I like this fringe for two reasons: first, it looks great, and second, I don't have to take my needle back up the length of the string! I especially like the look in very long fringe, but try a short sample first, using the same size seed beads that you'd use for a longer version of the fringe

Bring your needle out of the fabric and string on the number of beads you need for the length you want in any combination of colors. Add your end bead and then pick up exactly the same number of beads you have in the first half. If you have color changes, the second half should be a mirror image of the first half.

Before you take your needle back into the fabric, park it out of the way and grab the thread close to the last beads added. You are going to twist the thread in one direction so that when the needle goes back into the fabric the beads twist together. You can check this from time to time while you are twisting by laying the two halves together and twirling the end bead. If the two sides twist together and stay there, you are ready to take the needle back into the fabric and knot off.

Left sample shows what the string looked like before it was twisted.

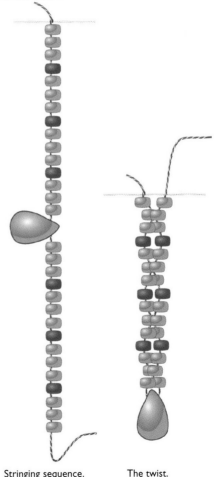

Stringing sequence.   The twist.

Edges

Basic Picot Edge

This is a lovely, simple edge for finishing a pin or medallion. To start, bring the needle out through the edge of the fabric. Pick up 3 beads. * Bring the needle towards you, taking a small stitch across the fold. The middle bead should stand up, resting on the other two (just like in moss stitch). Do not take the needle back into the fold. Bring the needle back up through the last bead again and add 2 beads. Repeat from * until you have completed the edge. If you are edging around a medallion or other form, when you get all the way around, you will need to add only 1 bead to close the circle.

The picot edge can be used as a device for assembling a small bag or doll. Simply fold over the fabric edges and stitch across the two folds together, using the beaded edge as the seam.

Completed picot edge circle.

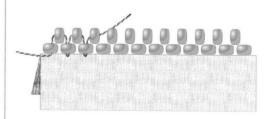

Thread path.

Final bead to close circle. *Indicated beginning of picot edge.

Picot Edge Variations

Once you have a picot edge in place, you can add additional rows of beads to create a variety of ruffles and decorative edges.

Variation 1.

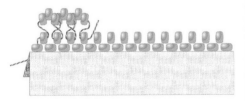

Thread path.

Variation 2.

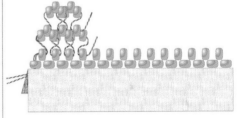

Thread path.

1. Bring the needle up so that you have passed through an "up" bead. Add 3 beads and pass through the next up bead. Repeat all the way around the shape.

2. For even more pizzazz, try adding a third row of 3 beads, using the center bead of the previous row as your guide, or up bead.

Variation 3.

Variation 4.

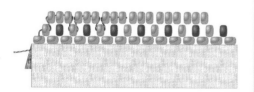

Thread path.

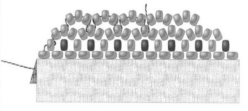

Thread path.

3. A smoother look can be achieved by adding 3 beads but passing through every other up bead.

4. And, of course, a third row can be added for a deeper ruffle.

Variation 5.

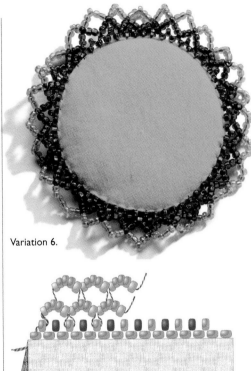

Variation 6.

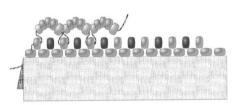

Thread path.

Thread path.

5. Now try upping the drama with a larger ruffle. Instead of 3 beads, add 5 beads, and pass through every other up bead.

6. And for the ultimate, add a third row of 5 beads, passing through the center bead of the previous row additions.

Variation 7.

Variation 8.

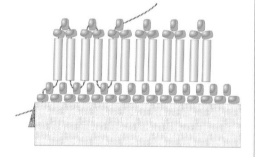

Thread path.

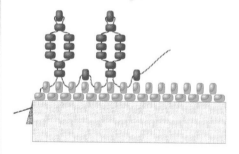

Thread path.

7. Bugle beads make a fun, wonky edge. As with all bugle bead uses, this is vulnerable to thread cutting. Use it on something that won't get a lot of handling. Bring the needle up out of 1 up bead, string 1 bugle, 3 seed beads, and 1 bugle. Skip over 1 up bead, and go through the following up bead. Continue around the circle.

8. Using the wonderful leaf shapes from leafy fringe makes a great edge. Add a leaf between every other up bead, or for good crunchy texture, between every up bead.

Variation 9.

Variation 10.

Thread path.

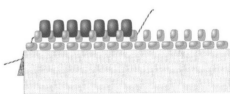

Thread path.

9. Teardrops can be used between up beads, if they are small enough. The larger ones will have to be added with seed beads on either side, skipping an up bead to accommodate the width that this will create.

10. For a very smooth edge, with just a hint of texture, make your picot edge with size 10° or 11° seed beads and add a contrasting size 8° seed bead between each up bead.

Variation 11.

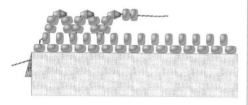

Thread path.

11. I love the glitz of faceted glass, and small bicones with seed beads on either side make a great sparkly edge. Bring the needle through an up bead, string on 2 or 3 seed beads, a faceted bead, and 2 or 3 more seed beads. Skip over one up bead, and take the needle into the following up bead. If you use very small (2mm) bicones, you might be able to go through every up bead with your additions.

Fused glass.

Fused glass.

Stone.

Fossil.

Cloisonné.

Blown glass.

Etched stone.

Stone donut.

Resin.

Various cabochons.

Caging the Wild Cabochon

Stacked Cage

The easiest and most flexible cage is done with stacks. Glue the cabochon in place and allow the glue to dry. Create stacks around the perimeter of the cabochon, using a larger (size 6° or so) bead at the bottom and size 11° beads on top of that. The stack should be tall enough that it can comfortably lean over the edge of the cabochon when pulled up tightly. If your cabochon is irregular in height, start at the tallest edge and use that as your guide. Better to be too tall than too short.

The stacks can be placed so that the base beads are almost touching or can be spaced out with up to ¼" between base beads. The space can be left open or filled later. When the stacks are completed, knot off your thread. If you're down to the last few inches of thread, now would be a good time to rethread your needle.

Bring your needle up all the way through one of the stacks. You will be adding small seed beads between the stacks. There is no magic number to this process. You want the stacks to lean in and cage the cabochon. Too few beads between stacks will leave thread showing. Too many beads

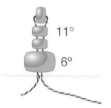

Basic stack.

Base bead should be close to, but not touching, the cabochon.

will make a loose cage from which the cabochon might escape should the glue let go. With irregularly shaped cabochons or irregularly spaced beads, you may need to vary how many beads are added between stacks.

When you have completed the circle, pull it up tight and check both the tension of the cage and to make sure you have no thread showing. Pass through a couple of sets of beads so that you are not taking your needle down through the same stack you came up through. It already has six strands of thread in it, and your needle may get stuck. Go back down through the stack, into the fabric, and knot off.

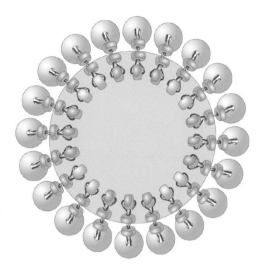

Base beads very close together.

Base beads spread out, and space between filled later.

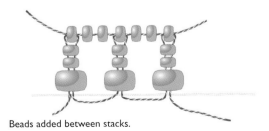

Beads added between stacks.

Lace Cage

This is a combination of backstitch and the picot edge lace. The base row is done as a modified backstitch. Bring the needle up close to the cabochon. Thread on 7 size 11° seed beads. Go back down into the fabric so that the beads make a nice arch. Pay attention to the distance between the first and last beads of the arch. * Bring the needle up that distance away from the first bead, still close to the cabochon and add 6 beads. Take the needle down through the first bead of the previous arch and into the fabric. That bead serves as the seventh bead of the second arch. Repeat from * all around the cabochon. For the final arch, you will add only 5 beads, since the 2 base beads will already be in place. It's a good idea to knot off at this point.

Now you will add additional arch rows, just as in the picot edge. Come up through the first 4 beads of a base row arch, and add 3 or 5 beads. How many beads you add and how many rows of arches you need will be determined by how tall your cabochon is; it may take a little experimenting.

Lace cage.

Once the cage is sufficient to entrap the cabochon, proceed to close any gaps as with the stacked cage; add beads between the arch points to draw them in, taking care to add enough to hide any thread and not so many as to make the cage useless.

First row of arches.

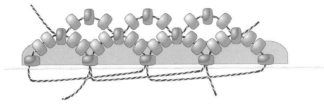

Second arch row: 3 beads between each arch.

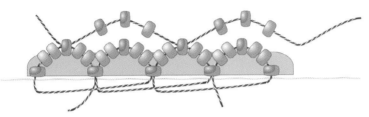

Second arch row: 3 beads every other arch (for very short cabochon).

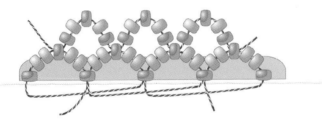

Second arch row: 5 beads between each arch (for taller cabochon).

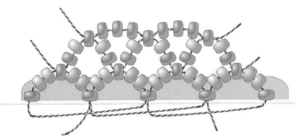

Third arch row: 3 beads between each arch to draw in the cage.

Gourd on the Ground

The stitch used for this cage is commonly called peyote or gourd stitch. I like it best when worked with Delica-style beads, but it will also work with regular seed beads.

Start with a base row of backstitch around the perimeter of the cabochon, taking care to end up with an even number of beads, even if you have to fudge a little at the end. (If you do your backstitch row in sets of four, you won't have to keep track.) Coming out of a bead, pick up 1 bead, then skip over the next bead on the base row and take the needle into and out of the following bead. The bead you just added should sit on top of the bead you skipped over. (This row can look pretty sloppy, but don't worry. The next row will neaten it right up.) Continue around the cabochon, adding 1 and skipping 1. It should look a bit like zipper teeth.

For the next row, bring the needle up through the first bead you added to the second row. Pick up a bead and pass through the next up bead. Continue around the cabochon, adding 1 bead between each up bead.

Continue adding rows until the wall of gourd stitch stands up above the top of the cabochon.

Gourd on the Ground with Delicas. Final row of 3 beads.

To draw the wall in and encase the cabochon, add a row around the top as follows: take the needle through an up bead, add 3 beads, skip 1 up bead, and pass through the following up bead. Continue around the cabochon, pull it up snug, and take the needle back down into the fabric behind the wall of beads, taking care not to let any of the thread show. Pass through whatever beads are necessary to do so.

If you are using a cabochon that has a fairly steep dome, you might find it more secure to use 5 beads instead of 3, and then gather the points together as in the lace cage.

Base backstitch row.

Second row: add 1, skip 1.

Third row: add 1 between each up bead.

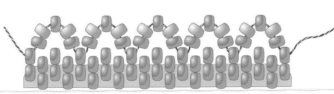

For shallow cabochon, add 3 beads, skip 1 up bead, pass through next up bead.

Gourd on the Ground with Delicas. Five beads used for drawing in and final row to gather top together.

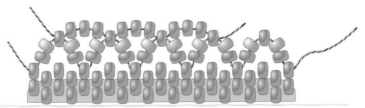

For steep cabochon, add 5 beads, skip 1 up bead, pass through next up bead.

To finish steep cabochon, add final row to draw arches in.

Assisi To Santiago De Compostela

6 × 3.25" + strap

Techniques: Encrusted beading, shell.

Statement: From my talisman collection, this piece was made to wear on a pilgramage that began in Assisi, Italy, and ended in Santiago de Compostela, Spain.

Candle Cloth

10.75" diameter

Techniques: Encrusted beading.

Statement: This cloth was designed to hold a pottery candleholder that was made for me by a friend. To ensure it would lay flat, it was worked on a frame.

Harvest Moon

21.75 × 19.75"

Techniques: Fused appliqué, machine quilting, beading, hot-fix charms.

Statement: This bold quilt will capture the viewer's attention and then draw them in to see the fine details of beads and charms.

Junk Jar Keyhole

11 × 8.5"

Techniques: Machine piecing, fused appliqué, machine quilted, beading.

Statement: When I get down to the last few beads of any type, they go into a jar rather than back into my organized bead storage. It's great fun to work without a plan with a pile of miscellaneous unmatched beads.

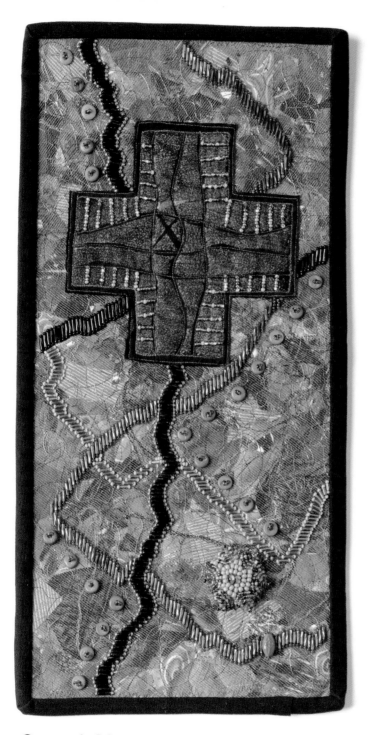

Crossroads: Advent

15 × 7.5"

Techniques: Fabric collage, machine quilting, beading, beaded button.

Statement: From the *Crossroads* series, which follows the liturgical calendar system of color. The color for *Advent* is blue, but I couldn't resist adding green to the mix.

Window Ala Gaudi

13.5 × 11"

Techniques: Fused appliqué, machine quilting, beading.

Statement: Inspired by the windows in The Güell Colony Crypt south of Barcelona, created by Antoni Gaudi.

Aftershock

16.5 × 8.75"

Techniques: Machine piecing, fused appliqué, machine quilting, beading.

Statement: This is how I feel after an earthquake! The scattered beading helps provide the feeling of motion and disorientation.

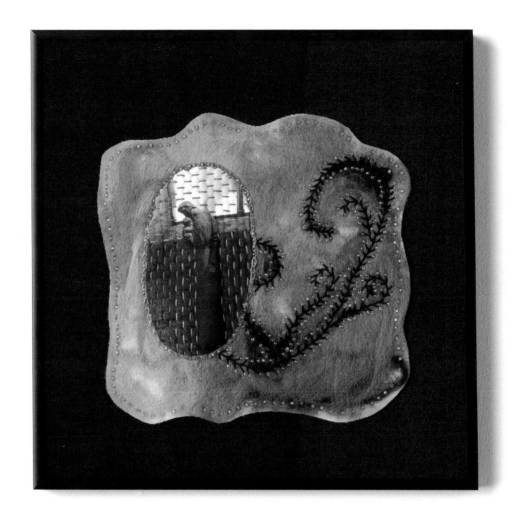

A Father's Care

(unfinished)

about 10 × 10"

Techniques: Needle-felted wool, photo transfer, hand embroidery, beading.

Statement: Minimal beading among the embroidery brings a glimmer of light to this soft piece inspired by a statue of father and child.

CHAPTER 5
Final Thoughts

In the course of teaching my beadwork classes, there are a few questions that regularly get asked. So, I thought I would include them here.

Painting Timtex

I have been using Timtex as a dimensional appliqué fabric for some time, as well as a backing for beading. Sometimes the Timtex is covered with fabric, but I also like painting the Timtex and using it as the fabric for beading. If the piece is going into a frame, you can just brush color onto the surface, do the beading, and pop it into the frame. But if the shapes will be cut out of the painted Timtex, you want the edges to be colored, not white.

Using plain acrylic paint, available at any craft store, dilute the paint with 5 parts water to 1 part paint. Mix this well, and keep mixing if it starts to settle while you are applying the paint. Use a sponge or brush and liberally apply the paint to the Timtex. Flip it over and apply the paint to

Painted Timtex with cabochons.

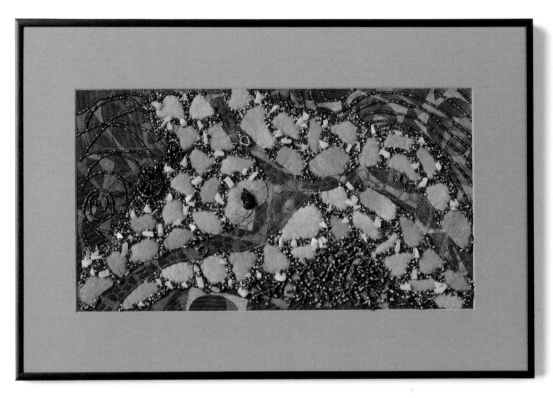

Dry Creek

(unfinished)

about 10 × 17"

Techniques: Fabric collage, machine quilting, painted Timtex, beading.

Statement: Inspired by a visit to a dry place in summer drought conditions where there was evidence that water had been in the area—but not recently.

the other side as well. You want to saturate the Timtex with paint. Then let it dry. In my corner of the world (the Pacific Northwest), this can take up to three days, but in drier climates it could be faster. You can speed up the process with a hair dryer or heat gun, but why not just go back to beading something else while it dries?

By the way, acrylic paint will ruin nail polish, so if you want to preserve your manicure, wear gloves for this process.

Framing

If your beadwork is going into a frame, you will want to plan for the additional fabric you will need for wrapping around the mounting board. I generally allow 2" all around the stitched area.

Once the beading is complete, you will need a piece of foam board cut to the size of the frame. Center your beadwork on the board, checking placement by pushing the edges down over the sides of the board. Stabilize the fabric with straight pins, which are pushed through the fabric and into the edges of the foam board. Pull the fabrics over the edges so that the fabric is tight against the board. This will keep the fabric from shifting as you lace the back.

When all the pins are in place, turn the board over so that the beadwork is face down on several layers of towels. The excess fabric will be pulled tight over the back of the board by lacing it in both directions. I use a size E or F Nymo for

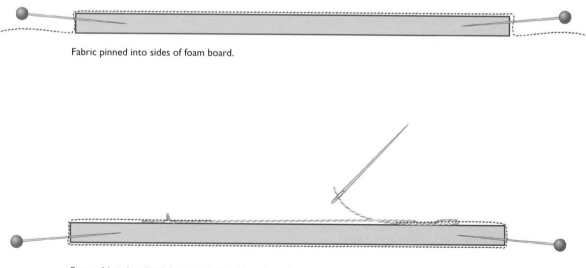

Fabric pinned into sides of foam board.

Excess fabric laced tightly across back of foam board.

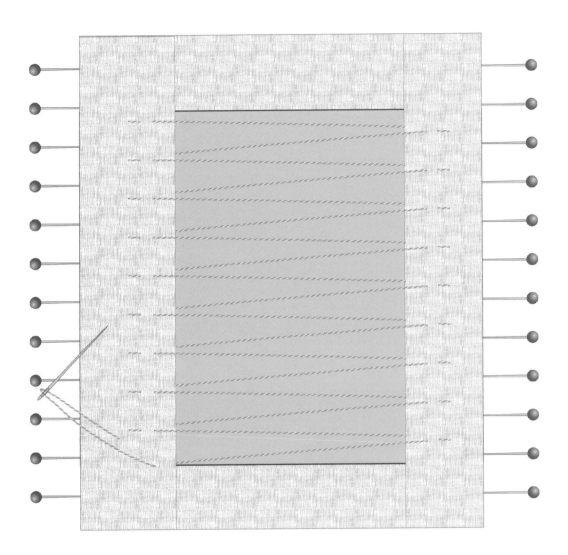

this task but a heavy carpet-weight thread will do very well. Starting at one corner, take a double stitch with the needle pointing toward the center of the board. Proceed to the other side and do likewise. Proceed down the entire length of the board in this manner, knotting off and starting new threads as needed. Make the stitches about an inch apart. Keep the tension very tight, or the fabric on the front will get sloppy.

Now proceed to lacing in the opposite direction in the same manner. When the

Fabric laced securely to foam board, and cabochon stabilized by stitching through board.

lacing is complete, you may remove all the straight pins. At this point, check the front of the piece to make sure everything is tight and secure.

If you have used a heavy cabochon, this would be the time to take some securing stitches to prevent sagging. Thread a heavy-weight needle (not a beading needle) with a thread that matches the fabric on the front and take several unobtrusive stitches through the foam board and around the cabochon. Keep your pliers nearby to help you pull the needle through the foam board. It also helps to push a pin through from the front so you have guide holes for the needle.

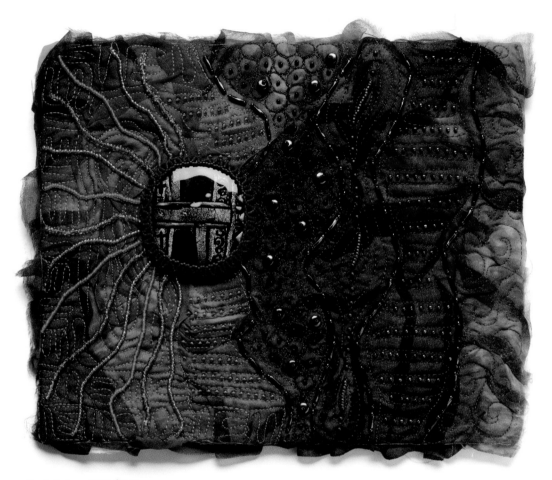

Ready to be put into frame.

Somehow you need to protect the lacing stitches from being snagged and possibly broken. I like to use mat board cut to the size of the frame, but a heavyweight poster board or even watercolor paper would do the job. It also provides you with a place to sign and date your work, if you prefer not to sign the front.

Finishing Medallions

I make a lot of beaded medallion necklaces, so my students always want to know how to finish the backs. I have experimented with a lot of different things, each having their own merits.

The first step is to trim away all but about ½" of the excess fabric when the beading is complete. Fold this in and stitch it to the batting or flannel that you used as a stabilizer. The stitching won't show, so don't worry about what thread color you use or the size of your stitches.

Many of my medallions are irregularly shaped, and the easiest way I have found of getting an accurate pattern for the backing piece is to put the medallion on the photocopy machine and shoot a picture of the back. Cut it out and you have a pattern.

If you want your medallion to retain some drape and softness, use a soft backing fabric that also has some wearability. The back is what will be rubbing against your clothing while you wear it, so a loose weave, lightweight fabric may not be your best choice. I like Ultrasuede for this purpose.

If you want your medallion to be more stable, you have several choices. Chip board is lightweight, inexpensive, and readily available but has one drawback. If you live in a humid climate or should your medallion get wet, the chip board will dissolve into a sodden lumpy mess. A scrap of Timtex or Lacy's Stiff Stuff will do the job very nicely. Lightweight plastic is also a good choice and is readily available at

fabric and quilt shops as template plastic. It's also less expensive than Timtex or Lacy's Stiff Stuff. Plastic canvas, found at craft shops, is also an alternative.

Cut your backing material to size (double check by laying it back to back on the medallion and trim as necessary) and then cut a piece of fabric ¾" larger all the way around. Take a basting stitch all around the outside edge of the fabric, a scant ¼" from the edge, and pull the thread up to gather the fabric around the backing material.

You can either stitch the medallion and backing together with invisible stitches or use the picot edge stitch to hold the two pieces together. And once the picot edge is in place, well, you might just as well add some ruffles!

A Great Outpouring

19.5 × 4.5" (21 × 6" framed)

Techniques: Hand-dyed and textured silk, machine
quilting, beading, fused-glass cabochon.

Statement: The long, lean line of this piece enhances
the feeling of a great outpouring of spirit and emotion.

Flood Plain

20 × 15.5"

Techniques: Fused appliqué, machine quilting, beading.

Statement: Winter ice on the flood plains of the Skagit Valley,
with the beading defining the whorls and fissures in the ice.

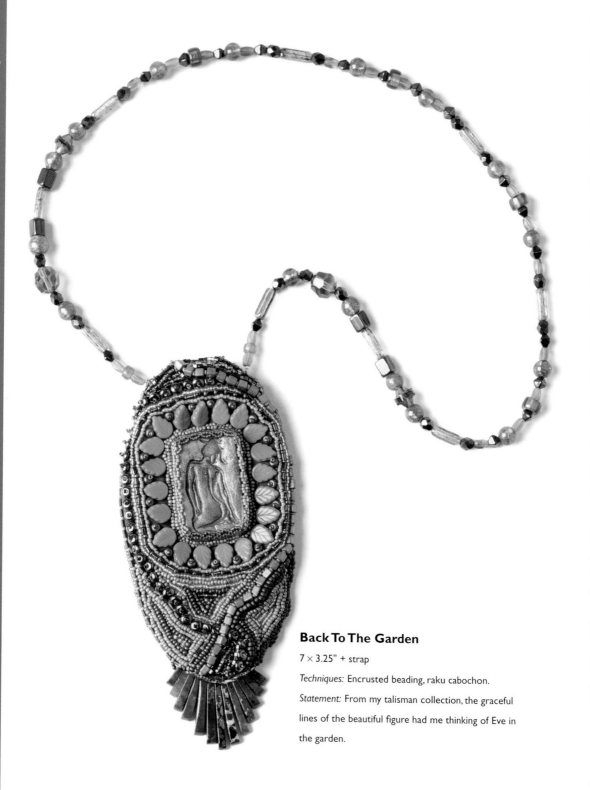

Back To The Garden

7 × 3.25" + strap

Techniques: Encrusted beading, raku cabochon.

Statement: From my talisman collection, the graceful lines of the beautiful figure had me thinking of Eve in the garden.

Baja Sunset

5 × 5" (8 × 8" framed)

Techniques: Encrusted beading, fused-glass cabochon.

Statement: I love the vivid colors of Mexico, which inspired this piece.

Resources

I strongly believe in supporting our local bead shops. (One look at my shelves, groaning under the weight of all that glass, will confirm this!) But not every shop can carry every possible item you might want to use. So here are a few online and catalog options to fill in the gaps.

Shipwreck Beads
8560 Commerce Place Dr. NE
Lacey, WA 98516
(360) 754-2323
www.shipwreck-beads.com
80,000 square feet of beads: seed beads, bugles, and pressed glass (primarily Czech, some Japanese), fire-polished and crystal beads, charms, findings, and books.

Fire Mountain Gems
One Fire Mountain Wy.
Grants Pass, OR 97526-2373
(800) 423-2319
www.firemountaingems.com
Seed beads, bugles, and pressed glass (Japanese, Czech, Chinese), Swarovski crystals, hill tribe silver, charms, findings, and books.

Beadcats
PO Box 2840
Wilsonville, OR 97070
(503) 625-2323
www.beadcats.com
Seed and bugle beads (Japanese), pressed glass (Czech), and every color of thread.

Caravan Beads and Fibers
915 Forest Ave.
Portland, ME 04103
(207) 761-2503
www.caravanbeads.com
Seed beads (Japanese), pearls, Swarovski crystals, and threads.

General Beads
317 National City Blvd.
National City, CA 91950-1110
(619) 336-0100
www.genbead.com
Seed and bugle beads (Japanese, Czech, Chinese), Swarovski crystals, charms, findings, and books.

San Francisco Arts & Crafts
1592 Union St.
Box 174
San Francisco, CA 94123
(707) 935-6756
www.sanfranciscoartscrafts.com
Large variety of bead soup assortments (seeds, bugles, cubes, etc., all in one color scheme).

Beyond Beadery
PO Box 460
Rollinsville, CO 80474
(303) 258-9389
www.beyondbeadery.com
Seed and bugle beads (Japanese, Czech), pressed glass (Czech), Swarovski crystals, threads, and storage boxes.

Out on a Whim
121 E. Cotati Ave.
Cotati, CA 94931
(707) 664-8343
www.whimbeads.com
Seed beads (Japanese), pressed glass (Czech), Swarovski crystals, charms, findings, books, and storage boxes.

Cartwrights (Sequins)
11108 N. Hwy. 348
Mountainburg, AR 72946
(479) 369-2074
www.ccartwright.com
Sequins.

Red Tail Glassworks
(Fused-glass cabochons)
5280 Bercot Rd.
Freeland, WA 98249
(360) 331-1205
www.redtailglassworks.com
Fused glass pendants and cabochons.

Index